A FatCat Book

THE KING OF CHRISTMAS

All God's Children Search for Jesus

Art by
Natasha Kennedy

Text by
Todd R. Hains

LEXHAM PRESS

HEAVENLY FATHER,

Thank you for giving us the light of your word.

It is the guiding star that leads us to your Son.

Send your Holy Spirit into our hearts,

so that we follow your word and

receive your Son. Through

Jesus Christ our

King.

AMEN.

What is FatCat?

FatCat is our way of making the catechism approachable. He represents the catechism: the Ten Commandments, the Apostles' Creed, and the Lord's Prayer.

In this book, FatCat guides us through the truth we celebrate on the Holy Day of Christmas. The magi found our Lord and King Jesus by the light of a star. Today we find our Lord and King Jesus by the light of his word. Follow FatCat and the magi as they journey over sea and field to Jerusalem, Bethlehem, and finally to Jesus.

FatCat is hidden throughout the pages of this book. Search for him with your child as you enjoy this book together, and hide the truth of Jesus in your heart.

The baby born in a manger is the God put to death on a cross and risen again from the dead. Wherever his name and word are, you will find him too.

Merry Christmas to all God's children!

"You, O LORD, are in the midst of us,
and we are called by your name."

Jeremiah 14:9

The heavens where the stars shine—
is the King of Christmas there?

No!

The sky where the birds fly—
is the King of Christmas there?

No!

The waters where the fish swim—
is the King of Christmas there?

No!

The fields where the beasts roam—
is the King of Christmas there?

No!

The tables where the rich eat—
is the King of Christmas there?
No!

The thrones where the mighty sit—
is the King of Christmas there?

No!

The market where the merchants sell—
is the King of Christmas there?

No!

The temple where the scribes teach—
is the King of Christmas there?

No!

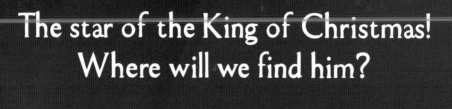

The star of the King of Christmas!
Where will we find him?

The manger where animals eat—
is the King of Christmas there?

Yes!

The cross where criminals die—
is the King of Christmas there?

Yes!

The grave where his body was laid—
is the King of Christmas there?

No!

PREACHING THE WORD

MARK 16:15

BAPTISM

MATT 28:19

THE LORD'S SUPPER

MATT 26:26–28

FORGIVENESS OF SINS

JOHN 20:22–23

The word, where he promises to be found—
is the King of Christmas there?
Yes!

Wherever his word and name are, you will find him too!

Families are little churches.

We pray together. We bring our sin and sadness, our joy and faith to the Lord our God. We read the Bible together. We hear Jesus' promises for us. And we forgive each other, because God, in Christ, has forgiven us.

This brief service of family prayer is designed to be prayed responsively. The leader reads the plain text; everyone reads the bold text. Even though your children might not be readers yet, they'll learn these words as you repeat them again and again each day. You could use it in the morning or evening—or anytime you and your children read this book, even if it's not Christmas time!

Christmas Prayer

In the name of the Father
and of the Son and of the Holy Spirit.
Amen.

A Child is born to us,
a Son is given to us.

Isaiah 9:6 NLT

All kings will bow before him,
and all nations will serve him.
He will rescue the poor when they cry to him;
he will help the oppressed,
who have no one to defend them.

Psalm 72:11–12 NLT

This is my only comfort in my trouble,
for your word has given me life.

Psalm 119:50 BCP

God has made us his people through our baptism into Christ. Living together in trust and hope, we confess our faith:

I believe in God, the Father almighty,
    maker of heaven and earth;
And in Jesus Christ, his only Son, our Lord;
    who was conceived by the Holy Spirit,
    born of the Virgin Mary,
    suffered under Pontius Pilate,
    was crucified, died, and was buried.
    He descended into hell.
    On the third day he rose again from the dead.
    He ascended into heaven,
    and is seated at the right hand of the Father.
    He will come again to judge
        the living and the dead.
I believe in the Holy Spirit,
    the holy catholic church,
    the communion of saints,
    the forgiveness of sins,
    the resurrection of the body,
    and the life everlasting.
Amen.

God is our loving Father.

He wants to hear our questions, fears, and joys.

Let us boldly offer our prayers for others
and for ourselves to God:

Parents, you might prompt your children's
prayers by asking questions like:

What are you thankful for?
What are you afraid of?
What do you want to tell God?

You might also pray the words of the Bible,
especially the Lord's Prayer, or the Apostles' Creed.
Make these words your own!

Heavenly Father,
thank you for giving us the light of your word.
It is the guiding star that leads us to your Son.
Send your Holy Spirit into our hearts,
so that we follow your word and receive your Son.
Through Jesus Christ our King. Amen.

Let us bless the LORD.

Thanks be to God.

The grace of our Lord Jesus Christ
and the love of God and the communion
of the Holy Spirit be with us all.   2 Corinthians 13:14

Amen.

To Parents

This book presents the story of the magi searching for baby Jesus, the King of Christmas (Matthew 2:1-12). The Bible connects Jesus' birth and death. Only the magi, Pontius Pilate, and Pilate's soldiers call Jesus "the King of the Jews." And so, when the magi ask Herod, "Where is he who has been born King of the Jews?" (Matthew 2:2), we can already picture the charge posted against him on the cross: "The King of the Jews." That's why this book continues the magi's search for Jesus to his death and resurrection.

Jesus is the one about whom the prophet Isaiah said: "A Child is born to us, a Son is given to us" (Isaiah 9:6 NLT). He is the word made flesh who gave himself on the cross to defeat death with his death, so you can have life, salvation, and the forgiveness of sins.

The Bible sets the center and boundary of this book's art. In addition to Matthew 2, the Psalms and Mary's Song (also called the Magnificat, Luke 1:46-55) help provide the places where the magi and FatCat search for the King of Christmas.

They start their search in nature. "The heavens declare the glory of God" (Psalm 19:1). So they search sky and heaven, land and water. But they don't find him. "His majesty is above earth and heaven" (Psalm 148:13).

They search human cities and dwellings. "You have made him a little lower than the heavenly beings and crowned him with glory and honor" (Psalm 8:5). So they search for him among the rich and noble, among soldiers and merchants, even among the religious leaders. They still don't find him. "He has brought down the mighty from their thrones. ... The rich he has sent away empty" (Luke 1:52-53).

Finally, they arrive in Bethlehem, a small, unknown place. And they search in unexpected places.

A feed box for cattle? And they find him!

A device for executing criminals? Yes, here he is again!

But the grave where they placed his body? No! "Why do you seek the living among the dead? He is not here, but has risen" (Luke 24:5-6).

So where is he now? In the word, where he promises to be: in the reading and proclamation of God's word, in baptism, in the Lord's Supper, and in the forgiveness of sins.

Jesus promises: "I am with you always" (Matthew 28:20).

The King of Christmas: All God's Children Search for Jesus
A FatCat Book

Copyright 2022 Natasha Kennedy / Lexham Press

Lexham Press, 1313 Commercial St., Bellingham, Washington 98225
LexhamPress.com

Printed in China.
ISBN 9781683596639
Library of Congress Control Number 2022932272

Lexham Editorial: Abigail Stocker, Kelsey Matthews, Lindsay John Kennedy,
    Veronica Hains
Cover Design: Natasha Kennedy

This book is typeset in FatCat.